ESSENTIAL DOCUMENT

GRAB 'N GO

ORGANIZER

ESSENTIAL DOCUMENT
GRAB 'N GO
ORGANIZER

THE **ULTIMATE GUIDE** TO
GATHERING:

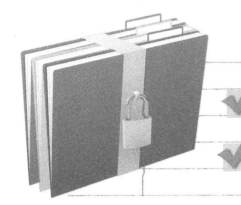

- ✔ **EMERGENCY CONTACTS**
- ✔ **PERSONAL & FINANCIAL RECORDS**
- ✔ **FAMILY INFORMATION**
- ✔ **AND OTHER VITAL DOCUMENTS**

HOBBLE CREEK PRESS
AN IMPRINT OF CEDAR FORT, INC.
SPRINGVILLE, UTAH

ISBN 13: 978-1-4621-1244-9

Published by Hobble Creek Press, an imprint of Cedar Fort, Inc.
2373 W. 700 S., Springville, UT 84663
Distributed by Cedar Fort, Inc., www.cedarfort.com

Cover and page design by Erica Dixon
Cover design © 2013 by Lyle Mortimer
Edited by Casey J. Winters

10 9 8 7 6 5 4 3 2 1

CONTENTS

CONTENTS

PREFACE

- Chernobyl, Ukraine
- Sendai, Japan
- Northridge, California
- South Lake Tahoe, California
- San Francisco, California
- Herriman, Utah
- New Orleans, Louisiana
- Mississippi River towns
- Santiago, Chile
- Joplin, Missouri

These are all sites of major disasters that have happened in the last thirty years. Have you ever given thought to what you would grab if you had twenty minutes to evacuate your home?

This idea/question came about while I was sitting in an insurance meeting discussing insurance losses, premiums, and loss ratios. In addressing these losses, someone noted that most of the time there was a disconnect between the insured who wanted immediate results and the adjuster trying to resolve a claim with little or no documentation. I perked up in the meeting and commented that we could do more to assist our insured clients through their insurance agent if more documentation was gathered before the policy was written. I suggested that our insurance agents meet at their clients' homes before writing their policy and take extensive pictures of the entire premises.

With almost twenty-five years of insurance experience, I have seen thousands of insurance losses and was either forced to make a quick decision, or, when time allowed, I would gather more critical information to make a more accurate payment. Along with my insurance background, I served for many years as my church's emergency preparedness coordinator. I worked with groups of at least one thousand people, trying to get them prepared in case of a disaster occurring in our community. With all my experience, I had the idea for the *Grab N Go Essential Document Organizer*.

Let me share with you some of my personal experiences with disasters that confirmed the need to create this organizer.

Herriman, Utah—Fire of 2010

September 19, 2010, started as a beautiful Sunday. My family and I were up early and getting ready for church when I went to let our dog outside. I thought I smelled smoke and told my husband. We proceeded to church and came home at about 2:00 p.m. Later in the afternoon, at approximately 5:30 p.m., we received a call from our friends who lived less than five minutes to the south of us to tell us they were being evacuated. They proceeded to tell us that the police department had come to their door telling them to gather what they could and evacuate immediately because the fire was coming over the hill. The fire and police departments had been notifying the Rose Canyon and Herriman Cove families. Upon receiving this call, we immediately went outside and looked to the south, where we could see dark smoke on the mountain. Within ten to fifteen minutes, we watched in shock as the fire crested the mountain and quickly took out the north side of it. This fire was fanned by the canyon winds, causing it to spread rapidly in our direction as well as eastward. It was out of control.

In the next few hours, we saw many horse trailers coming out of Rose Canyon with people trying to save their animals and any possessions they could grab. In the midst of the exodus, people were hoping to leave their animals at Butterfield Park; however, when they realized the enormity of this fire, most people had to take their animals to South Jordan Equestrian Park for safety.

It was a long night. We could see the planes with fire retardant flying overhead, trying desperately to save homes from Rose Canyon all the way east to the Rose Crest development. We could also see the lights of fire trucks and police vehicles trying to secure areas. Instead of getting our belongings together, we watched in a frozen state of mind. We worried about the fire jumping the road with the realization that we would need to get out quickly. I thought at the time I would grab my scrapbooks, my special items in my curio cabinet, clothes, and some of our personal documents. However, in horror I realized that I did not know which box in the garage contained our personal documents. We had only lived in our brand-new home for two months when this fire occurred, and I was not organized enough to know which box had the information. Besides worrying about our belongings, we could not call out on our home phone because it was dead, and our cell phones only worked sporadically. Ultimately we did not have to evacuate. In the aftermath, I spoke with our friends who were evacuated. Those who were pre-pared grabbed hard drives with their personal information, binders with some documentation, personal belongings, and pictures. Unfortunately over five thousand people were displaced for at least three days. Ten thousand acres burned in the fire, and four homes were lost. These families left for a few days and came back to nothing. I can only imagine how long it would take to recover their personal belongings and important papers and replace their home and possessions. It would take months to recuperate your social security card and any other important documents. To make matters more intense, you have to show some documentation or proof of losses to your insurance companies. I am sure it was very difficult for these people to remember every item they owned. Some of the insurance claims that came about from this fire took well over a year to completely resolve.

This experience made me wish I would have been more prepared with keeping our most important documents together. Even with years of preparation, I had not taken the time to gather all of these docu-ments. Now that I have completed my own organizer, I feel secure knowing that this information would save me many hours, days, and months of work in the event of another disaster.

Herriman, Utah—Fire of 2012

Within two short years we experienced our second major fire, but this time we were on our way to Idaho for a family reunion. We were just about to Tremonton, Utah, when our cell phones started to ring. I answered my phone, and it was my niece telling me that a fire had just started up the canyon from our home and it was moving fast. The next call came from our neighbors; they explained that they had walked up the hill and were watching the fire closely. I tried to convince my husband to turn around; however, even if we would have driven back, we would have been lucky to get to our neighborhood.

My neighbors watched as this fire came down Rose Canyon and continued down the west side of the Herriman Cove community. Ultimately the fire destroyed three homes, caused damage to many others, and consumed more than four thousand acres. Once again there was a mandatory evacuation—authori-ties evacuated more than 1600 people.

As the fire blazed, I continued to call my neighbors to receive reports on what was happening. This was the second disastrous fire to occur in a short span, and this time I had left my home and all my possessions. So what did I learn from my second major fire in less than two years? I realized the importance of having more than one information binder—I needed one at home and one stored away from my home in case a fire or some other disaster took my home.

Grab N Go Essential Document Organizer will help you gather all your important emergency contacts, individual family information, personal documents, photographs, pets and animal information, emergency funds, funeral preparation, and emergency plans before the next disaster occurs, which could be in your backyard—just like it was in mine!

I recommend transferring all copies of personal documents and the written information in this organizer to a separate binder. Purchase the following items to complete your project: a two-inch binder, clear plastic page protectors, a package of clear CD/DVD adhesive sleeves, burnable CDs or DVDs, and a disposable camera for pictures of personal possessions. Tear out the information pages in this organizer and put in page protectors. With regards to CD/DVD sleeves, place one in the front inside cover of your binder for your personal possessions CD. Below this sleeve, place another one to hold your extra keys to your cars or house. Additional CDs or DVDs could contain your past five years of taxes and other electronic documentation.

Keep the binder in a special spot at all times: a bookcase in your office or your family room near your photo albums. Do not label the outside of the binder—in this case, in the event of a robbery, the burglars would not know about the binder and its contents. If you do label the binder, use a code word on it that only you and other immediate family members know what it means.

Also, I recommend you have a separate binder with the original information, such as birth and marriage certificates, stored in a safe-deposit box at your local bank or with a trusted family member. Make sure this family member lives a lengthy distance away so they are not involved in the same disaster, and make sure that location will be a safe spot for your information.

During disasters, emotions are high, and it is hard to make sound decisions. My hope is that gathering the information to complete your binder will bring you peace of mind and a sense of security.

—Mary Rowbury

EMERGENCY CONTACTS

☐ **Emergency Contacts**

☐ **Other Emergency Contacts**

EMERGENCY CONTACT INFORMATION

In this section you will document your emergency contacts' information.

You should have these emergency contacts written down because, in the event of an emergency, you probably won't remember important numbers. In the event of a disaster, you will possibly be out of power and cell phone service. Most of us rely on the contact lists in our cell phones or on our home phones for these numbers. If we are left without power, we will have to depend on older phones that do not require electricity, and we will not have these important contact numbers handy.

In the Herriman Fire of 2010, we found that the cell phones were overloaded, and we could only call out on a limited basis. I remember calling my boss, who lived just east of us in Draper, and I could not get through. He could see that I had called; however, he could not get through to me until 7:00 a.m. the next morning.

During this fire, my husband ran down the hill to the church to try to assist our church leaders with further evacuations and to make sure the families were safe. He was able to call me using an older land-line, but his cell phone was not working. Keep in mind he knew our home phone number, but, if needed, he would not have known any other contact numbers except that of his parents, who live in Idaho.

If a crisis or major disaster strikes, adrenaline will set in, and you will more than likely not be able to remember personal emergency numbers. And 9-1-1 will likely be overloaded with calls. So it is important to have your family/friends emergency contact numbers as well as the current numbers and addresses for the local hospital, your doctor, the police department, the fire department, the power company, the water company, and so on.

Finally, make sure you have contacts out of the area you can call. In a crisis you will be more able to call out of the area versus down the road. In your family emergency plan, have a specific out-of-area contact to get in touch with and let them know you are okay. That way, if you are separated from your family, you can contact them and they will know you are safe.

EMERGENCY CONTACTS
Addresses and Phone Numbers

EMERGENCY CONTACT INFORMATION

Name

Relationship

Address

Street Address

City

State/Province

Postal/Zip Code

Phone Number   -   -

Cell Phone Number   -   -

EMERGENCY CONTACT INFORMATION

Name

Relationship

Address

Street Address

City

State/Province

Postal/Zip Code

Phone Number   -   -

Cell Phone Number   -   -

EMERGENCY CONTACT INFORMATION

Name

Relationship

Address

Street Address

City

State/Province

Postal/Zip Code

Phone Number   -   -

Cell Phone Number   -   -

EMERGENCY CONTACT INFORMATION

Name   Relationship

Address

Street Address

City   State/Province   Postal/Zip Code

Phone   -   -   Cell Phone   -   -
Number   Number

EMERGENCY CONTACT INFORMATION

Name   Relationship

Address

Street Address

City   State/Province   Postal/Zip Code

Phone   -   -   Cell Phone   -   -
Number   Number

EMERGENCY CONTACT INFORMATION

Name   Relationship

Address

Street Address

City   State/Province   Postal/Zip Code

Phone   -   -   Cell Phone   -   -
Number   Number

EMERGENCY CONTACT INFORMATION

Name   Relationship

Address

     Street Address

     City   State/Province   Postal/Zip Code

Phone
Number   -   -   Cell Phone
Number   -   -

EMERGENCY CONTACT INFORMATION

Name   Relationship

Address

     Street Address

     City   State/Province   Postal/Zip Code

Phone
Number   -   -   Cell Phone
Number   -   -

EMERGENCY CONTACT INFORMATION

Name   Relationship

Address

     Street Address

     City   State/Province   Postal/Zip Code

Phone
Number   -   -   Cell Phone
Number   -   -

OTHER EMERGENCY CONTACTS
Addresses and Phone Numbers

HOSPITAL INFORMATION

Name

Address

Street Address

City   State/Province   Postal/Zip Code

Phone
Number   –   –

AMBULANCE INFORMATION

Phone
Number   –   –

PRIMARY CARE PHYSICIAN INFORMATION

Name

Address

Street Address

City   State/Province   Postal/Zip Code

Phone
Number   –   –

POLICE DEPARTMENT INFORMATION

Address

Street Address

City   State/Province   Postal/Zip Code

Phone
Number   –   –

FIRE DEPARTMENT INFORMATION

Address

Street Address

City   State/Province   Postal/Zip Code

Phone
Number   ___ - ___ - ___

GAS COMPANY INFORMATION

Name

Phone
Number   ___ - ___ - ___

POWER COMPANY INFORMATION

Name

Phone
Number   ___ - ___ - ___

WATER COMPANY INFORMATION

Name

Phone
Number   ___ - ___ - ___

POISON CONTROL INFORMATION

Name

Phone
Number   ___ - ___ - ___

FAMILY INFORMATION

☐ **Family Information Sheet**

☐ **Individual Family Member Information Sheets**

☐ **Marriage Certificate**

☐ **Birth Certificates**

☐ **Social Security Cards**

☐ **Medical Issues**

☐ **Driver's Licenses**

☐ **Passports**

FAMILY INFORMATION

☐ Family Information Sheet

In this section you will document immediate family names, addresses, and pictures of your family and home. If a major crisis or disaster occurs, your family could be separated. For example, during the Salt Lake City tornado that occurred on August 11, 1999, at approximately 1:00 p.m., I was working downtown on the eighth floor of the First Security Bank building when this tornado—rated an F2—occurred. This crisis basically shut down the center of Salt Lake City, damaging over one hundred twenty homes and destroying thirty-four homes. I was five months pregnant at the time, and I would take the commuter bus to and from work. Since I lived at least twenty-five miles away from the office, I was worried how I was going to get home. It took a lot longer to get a bus home that night due to traffic congestion of people trying to get out of the downtown area. What if I did not make it home that night? With limited phone access, I could have been displaced, hurt, or even missing.

- With this family information sheet, you have a list of your immediate family and their names as well as current pictures of the family and the home. In a missing-person situation, you could provide the necessary information to assist in finding a lost family member.

☐ Individual Family Member Information Sheets

In this section you will document extensive information on each member of your family: personal, employment or school, medical, dental, and health insurance information. You should also keep copies of legal documents here, such as social security cards, birth certificates, passports, copies of driver's licenses, immunization records, medical histories if available, blood types, and current medications. Additional vital documents would be adoption papers, citizenship papers, divorce paperwork, and so on. I recommended that you update pictures of adults once a year and children every six months. I also recommend that you update this binder when you need to make changes to any information.

- Place a hair sample in plastic bag for DNA in each family member's section. This documentation is extremely important—if you lose your social security card or birth certificate, it will take months to recuperate this information. Under federal law, you have to show proof of this information to get a driver's license, and you also have to show employers this information to get a job.

FAMILY
Information Sheet

Family Name

Address

Street Address

City   State/Province   Postal/Zip Code

Adult's Name   Adult's Name

Home Phone
Number   –   –   Number of
Children

Children's Names

Picture of Family   Picture of Home

ADULT EMERGENCY
Information Sheet

PHOTO

Name

Date of Birth

Place of Birth

Social Security
Number

Cell Phone
Number

Height   Weight

Hair Color   Eye Color   Glasses   Y / N   Skin Tone
                                                 Contacts   Y / N

Birthmarks/
Scars

Profession   Place of
                                                 Employment

Employment
Address

Street Address

City   State/Province   Postal/Zip Code

Work Phone
Number

MEDICAL INFORMATION

Blood Type

Physician   Phone
                                                 Number

Address

Street Address

City   State/Province   Postal/Zip Code

Fingerprints
(use black ink pad)

Left   Right

Allergies

Medical
Conditions

Medications

DENTAL INFORMATION

Dentist

Phone Number   -   -

Address

Street Address

City   State/Province   Postal/Zip Code

Teeth
Missing

Dentures   Y / N   Braces   Y / N   Permanent Retainers   Y / N

DNA HAIR SAMPLE (IN A PLASTIC BAG)

Date   -   -

HEALTH INSURANCE INFORMATION

Health Insurance
Provider

Phone Number   -   -

Policy
Number

Group
Number

ADULT EMERGENCY
Information Sheet

PHOTO

Name

Date of Birth ___ - ___ - ___

Place of Birth

Social Security Number ___ - ___ - ___

Cell Phone Number ___ - ___ - ___

Height   Weight

Hair Color   Eye Color   Glasses   Y / N   Skin Tone
                                           Contacts   Y / N

Birthmarks/ Scars

Profession   Place of Employment

Employment Address

Street Address

City   State/Province   Postal/Zip Code

Work Phone Number ___ - ___

MEDICAL INFORMATION

Blood Type

Physician   Phone Number ___ - ___

Address

Street Address

City   State/Province   Postal/Zip Code

Fingerprints
(use black ink pad)

Left   Right

Allergies

Medical
Conditions

Medications

DENTAL INFORMATION

Dentist

Phone
Number   —   —

Address

Street Address

City   State/Province   Postal/Zip Code

Teeth
Missing

Dentures   Y / N   Braces   Y / N   Permanent Retainers   Y / N

DNA HAIR SAMPLE (IN A PLASTIC BAG)

Date   —   —

HEALTH INSURANCE INFORMATION

Health Insurance
Provider

Phone
Number   —   —

Policy
Number

Group
Number

CHILD EMERGENCY
Information Sheet

PHOTO

Name

Date of Birth   –   –

Place of Birth

Social Security
Number   –   –

Cell Phone
Number   –   –

Height   Weight

Hair Color   Eye Color

Glasses   Y / N
Contacts   Y / N   Skin Tone

Birthmarks/
Scars

School

School
Address

Street Address

City   State/Province   Postal/Zip Code

School Phone
Number   –   –

MEDICAL INFORMATION

Blood Type

Physician   Phone
Number   –   –

Address

Street Address

City   State/Province   Postal/Zip Code

Fingerprints
(use black ink pad)

Left   Right

Allergies

Medical
Conditions

Medications

DENTAL INFORMATION

Dentist

Phone
Number   -   -

Address

Street Address

City   State/Province   Postal/Zip Code

Teeth
Missing

Dentures   Y / N   Braces   Y / N   Permanent Retainers   Y / N

DNA HAIR SAMPLE (IN A PLASTIC BAG)

Date   -   -

HEALTH INSURANCE INFORMATION

Health Insurance
Provider

Phone
Number   -   -

Policy
Number

Group
Number

CHILD EMERGENCY
Information Sheet

PHOTO

Name

Date of Birth   -   -

Place of Birth

Social Security
Number   -   -

Cell Phone
Number   -   -

Height   Weight

Hair Color   Eye Color   Glasses   Y / N   Skin Tone
                                                 Contacts   Y / N

Birthmarks/
Scars

School

School
Address

Street Address

City   State/Province   Postal/Zip Code

School Phone
Number   -   -

MEDICAL INFORMATION

Blood Type

Physician   Phone
                                      Number   -   -

Address

Street Address

City   State/Province   Postal/Zip Code

29

Fingerprints
(use black ink pad)

Left   Right

Allergies

Medical
Conditions

Medications

DENTAL INFORMATION

Dentist

Phone
Number — —

Address

Street Address

City   State/Province   Postal/Zip Code

Teeth
Missing

Dentures   Y / N   Braces   Y / N   Permanent Retainers   Y / N

DNA HAIR SAMPLE (IN A PLASTIC BAG)

Date — —

HEALTH INSURANCE INFORMATION

Health Insurance
Provider

Phone
Number — —

Policy
Number

Group
Number

CHILD EMERGENCY
Information Sheet

PHOTO

Name

Date of Birth   -   -

Place of Birth

Social Security
Number   -   -

Cell Phone
Number   -   -

Height   Weight

Hair Color   Eye Color

Glasses	Y / N
Contacts	Y / N

Skin Tone

Birthmarks/
Scars

School

School
Address

Street Address

City   State/Province   Postal/Zip Code

School Phone
Number   -   -

MEDICAL INFORMATION

Blood Type

Physician   Phone
Number   -   -

Address

Street Address

City   State/Province   Postal/Zip Code

Fingerprints
(use black ink pad)

Left   Right

Allergies

Medical
Conditions

Medications

DENTAL INFORMATION

Dentist

Phone
Number   -   -

Address

     Street Address

     City   State/Province   Postal/Zip Code

Teeth
Missing

Dentures   Y / N   Braces   Y / N   Permanent Retainers   Y / N

DNA HAIR SAMPLE (IN A PLASTIC BAG)

Date   -   -

HEALTH INSURANCE INFORMATION

Health Insurance
Provider

Phone
Number   -   -

Policy
Number

Group
Number

35

CHILD EMERGENCY
Information Sheet

PHOTO

Name

Date of Birth ___ - ___ - ___

Place of Birth

Social Security Number ___ - ___ - ___

Cell Phone Number ___ - ___ - ___

Height   Weight

Hair Color   Eye Color   Glasses   Y / N   Skin Tone
                                           Contacts   Y / N

Birthmarks/
Scars

School

School
Address

Street Address

City   State/Province   Postal/Zip Code

School Phone
Number ___ - ___ - ___

MEDICAL INFORMATION

Blood Type

Physician   Phone
                                             Number ___ - ___ - ___

Address

Street Address

City   State/Province   Postal/Zip Code

Fingerprints
(use black ink pad)

Left   Right

Allergies

Medical
Conditions

Medications

DENTAL INFORMATION

Dentist

Phone
Number   -   -

Address

    Street Address

    City   State/Province   Postal/Zip Code

Teeth
Missing

Dentures   Y / N   Braces   Y / N   Permanent Retainers   Y / N

DNA HAIR SAMPLE (IN A PLASTIC BAG)

Date   -   -

HEALTH INSURANCE INFORMATION

Health Insurance
Provider

Phone
Number   -   -

Policy
Number

Group
Number

HOME AND AUTO INFORMATION

☐ **Home and Auto Information Sheet**

☐ **Homeowners Insurance Declaration Page**

☐ **Previous Year's Mortgage Statement**

☐ **Deed to Home**

☐ **Title on Vehicles**

☐ **Auto Insurance Declaration Page**

HOME AND AUTO INFORMATION

In this section you will document information pertaining to your home, auto-mobiles, and other vehicles. Include mortgage company contact information, lienholder contact information for vehicles, and home and auto insurance contact information.

Also keep in this section:

☐ A copy of your homeowners insurance declaration page.

☐ A copy of last year's mortgage statement.

☐ A copy of the deed to your home, if you are the homeowner.

☐ A copy of all owned vehicle titles.

☐ Copies of your auto insurance declaration pages (update every six months). Also include pictures of your vehicles to show their stated condition.

Ultimately it is your responsibility to prove your claim to your insurance company. With this information at your fingertips, it should make for an easier process.

In the event a disaster takes place, you will immediately have the information to call your home or auto insurance to make a claim. Additionally, you will have your declarations pages available to see most of your coverages. With the South Lake Tahoe Fire, many homes and cars were lost. Most of us are required to have proof of insurance in our vehicles; however, if your vehicle is burned, you will need to have other immediate proof.

I highly recommend you review your home insurance coverages with your insurance agent once a year, or if you change insurance companies. For this organizer, include photos of each room in your home to help document your belongings in case of a total loss—this will help you remember what you had. This is discussed further in the personal belongings section.

HOME AND AUTO
Information Sheet

Address of
Home

Street Address

City   State/Province   Postal/Zip Code

Do you own your home?   Y / N

MORTGAGE INFORMATION

If you have a mortgage on your home, complete the following. Otherwise attach a copy of your deed in this section.

Mortgage
Company

Account Number
(last 4 digits)

Address

Street Address

City   State/Province   Postal/Zip Code

Phone Number   –   –

HOMEOWNERS INSURANCE INFORMATION

Homeowners
Insurance

Policy Number

Address

Street Address

City   State/Province   Postal/Zip Code

Phone Number   –   –

Agent's Name   Phone Number   –   –

AUTO INFORMATION

Year _____   Make _____   Model _____   Color _____

VIN _____

Lienholder
Name _____

Account
Number _____   Phone Number ___ – ___ – ___

Address _____

Street Address

_____

City _____   State/Province _____   Postal/Zip Code _____

AUTO INFORMATION

Year _____   Make _____   Model _____   Color _____

VIN _____

Lienholder
Name _____

Account
Number _____   Phone Number ___ – ___ – ___

Address _____

Street Address

_____

City _____   State/Province _____   Postal/Zip Code _____

AUTO INFORMATION

Year   Make   Model   Color

VIN

Lienholder
Name

Account   Phone Number   -   -
Number

Address

Street Address

City   State/Province   Postal/Zip Code

AUTO INFORMATION

Year   Make   Model   Color

VIN

Lienholder
Name

Account   Phone Number   -   -
Number

Address

Street Address

City   State/Province   Postal/Zip Code

AUTO INFORMATION

Year   Make   Model   Color

VIN

Lienholder
Name

Account
Number   Phone Number   –   –

Address

Street Address

City   State/Province   Postal/Zip Code

AUTO INFORMATION

Year   Make   Model   Color

VIN

Lienholder
Name

Account
Number   Phone Number   –   –

Address

Street Address

City   State/Province   Postal/Zip Code

OTHER VEHICLE INFORMATION

Type of
Vehicle

Year   Make   Model   Color

VIN

OTHER VEHICLE INFORMATION

Type of
Vehicle

Year   Make   Model   Color

VIN

OTHER VEHICLE INFORMATION

Type of
Vehicle

Year   Make   Model   Color

VIN

OTHER VEHICLE INFORMATION

Type of
Vehicle

Year   Make   Model   Color

VIN

PERSONAL TAX INFORMATION

☐ **Accountant Information**

☐ **Five Years of Taxes**

☐ **Electronic Tax Documentation**

PERSONAL TAX INFORMATION

☐ **In this section you will enter your accountant's information.**

☐ **Keep copies of your last five years of personal taxes in this section.** I recommend this because, in the case of a disaster, you could lose all your paper documents. After a disaster takes place, you could be replacing your home, and, if the insurance company does not process claims promptly, you are left to make your own financial arrangements. If you have to apply for a loan, you will need proof of income and taxes. Unfortunately, if these papers were lost, the government would take weeks or even months to send copies. I say *government* because your local tax consultant could have gone through the same disaster, and, depending on his backup plan, he could have also lost everything.

☐ **Another recommendation is to keep electronic documentation of each year of taxes.** Scan your tax documents and download them onto a CD. Keep the CD in this section for quick access.

ACCOUNTANT INFORMATION

Accountant
Name

Name of
Company

Address

Street Address

City   State/Province   Postal/Zip Code

Phone Number   -   -

ONLINE TAX SERVICES (IF APPLICABLE)

Name of
Company

Website

Username   Password

Year started
filing taxes with
this company

PERSONAL FINANCES INFORMATION

☐ **Personal Account Information Sheet**

☐ **Investments Information Sheet**

☐ **Credit Cards Information Sheet**

PERSONAL FINANCES INFORMATION

In this section you will list all your account information: bank, savings, checking, credit cards, IRA and investment, and children's savings.

- In the event of a crisis, there will more than likely be a lot of confusion until the situation settles. With this confused state comes stress and a lack of being able to remember important accounts and passwords.

- Let's look at the worst-case scenario: if the husband or the wife who was the main finance planner in your family died due to an unexpected event. Likely the other person will not know which bank has the money or where the investments may be.

- It is important to have a list of your credits cards in the event of a death to contact those companies and close those accounts, alleviating the possibility of someone else obtaining the credit information. Additionally, often the next of kin is unaware of unclaimed monies from people who have passed.

- Those who have children's savings accounts should have some documentation in the event of both parents' passing.

PERSONAL ACCOUNT
Information Sheet
Types of accounts: savings, checking, bank loans, children's savings, IRA/retirement savings

PERSONAL ACCOUNT INFORMATION

Account Type   Account Number

Financial
Institution

Address

    Street Address

    City   State/Province   Postal/Zip Code

Phone Number   -   -   Website

Username   Password

PERSONAL ACCOUNT INFORMATION

Account Type   Account Number

Financial
Institution

Address

    Street Address

    City   State/Province   Postal/Zip Code

Phone Number   -   -   Website

Username   Password

PERSONAL ACCOUNT INFORMATION

Account Type _____ Account Number _____

Financial
Institution _____

Address _____

Street Address

_____

City   State/Province   Postal/Zip Code

Phone Number _____ - _____ - _____ Website _____

Username _____ Password _____

PERSONAL ACCOUNT INFORMATION

Account Type _____ Account Number _____

Financial
Institution _____

Address _____

Street Address

_____

City   State/Province   Postal/Zip Code

Phone Number _____ - _____ - _____ Website _____

Username _____ Password _____

PERSONAL ACCOUNT INFORMATION

Account Type

Account Number

Financial
Institution

Address

Street Address

City

State/Province

Postal/Zip Code

Phone Number   –   –

Website

Username

Password

PERSONAL ACCOUNT INFORMATION

Account Type

Account Number

Financial
Institution

Address

Street Address

City

State/Province

Postal/Zip Code

Phone Number   –   –

Website

Username

Password

PERSONAL ACCOUNT INFORMATION

Account Type   Account Number

Financial
Institution

Address

Street Address

City   State/Province   Postal/Zip Code

Phone Number   –   –   Website

Username   Password

PERSONAL ACCOUNT INFORMATION

Account Type   Account Number

Financial
Institution

Address

Street Address

City   State/Province   Postal/Zip Code

Phone Number   –   –   Website

Username   Password

64

PERSONAL ACCOUNT INFORMATION

Account Type

Account Number

Financial
Institution

Address

Street Address

City   State/Province   Postal/Zip Code

Phone Number   –   –   Website

Username   Password

PERSONAL ACCOUNT INFORMATION

Account Type

Account Number

Financial
Institution

Address

Street Address

City   State/Province   Postal/Zip Code

Phone Number   –   –   Website

Username   Password

PERSONAL ACCOUNT INFORMATION

Account Type   Account Number

Financial
Institution

Address

Street Address

City   State/Province   Postal/Zip Code

Phone Number   –   –   Website

Username   Password

PERSONAL ACCOUNT INFORMATION

Account Type   Account Number

Financial
Institution

Address

Street Address

City   State/Province   Postal/Zip Code

Phone Number   –   –   Website

Username   Password

PERSONAL ACCOUNT INFORMATION

Account Type   Account Number

Financial
Institution

Address

Street Address

City   State/Province   Postal/Zip Code

Phone Number   −   −   Website

Username   Password

PERSONAL ACCOUNT INFORMATION

Account Type   Account Number

Financial
Institution

Address

Street Address

City   State/Province   Postal/Zip Code

Phone Number   −   −   Website

Username   Password

PERSONAL ACCOUNT INFORMATION

Account Type   Account Number

Financial
Institution

Address

Street Address

City   State/Province   Postal/Zip Code

Phone Number   –   –   Website

Username   Password

PERSONAL ACCOUNT INFORMATION

Account Type   Account Number

Financial
Institution

Address

Street Address

City   State/Province   Postal/Zip Code

Phone Number   –   –   Website

Username   Password

CREDIT CARDS
Information Sheet

CREDIT CARD INFORMATION

Account/
Card Number   PIN

Company

Address

Street Address

City   State/Province   Postal/Zip Code

Phone Number   –   –

CREDIT CARD INFORMATION

Account/
Card Number   PIN

Company

Address

Street Address

City   State/Province   Postal/Zip Code

Phone Number   –   –

69

CREDIT CARD INFORMATION

Account/
Card Number   PIN

Company

Address

Street Address

City   State/Province   Postal/Zip Code

Phone Number   –   –

CREDIT CARD INFORMATION

Account/
Card Number   PIN

Company

Address

Street Address

City   State/Province   Postal/Zip Code

Phone Number   –   –

CREDIT CARD INFORMATION

Account/
Card Number   PIN

Company

Address

Street Address

City   State/Province   Postal/Zip Code

Phone Number   –   –

CREDIT CARD INFORMATION

Account/
Card Number   PIN

Company

Address

Street Address

City   State/Province   Postal/Zip Code

Phone Number   -   -

CREDIT CARD INFORMATION

Account/
Card Number   PIN

Company

Address

Street Address

City   State/Province   Postal/Zip Code

Phone Number   -   -

CREDIT CARD INFORMATION

Account/
Card Number   PIN

Company

Address

Street Address

City   State/Province   Postal/Zip Code

Phone Number   -   -

CREDIT CARD INFORMATION

Account/
Card Number   PIN

Company

Address

Street Address

City   State/Province   Postal/Zip Code

Phone Number   –   –

CREDIT CARD INFORMATION

Account/
Card Number   PIN

Company

Address

Street Address

City   State/Province   Postal/Zip Code

Phone Number   –   –

CREDIT CARD INFORMATION

Account/
Card Number   PIN

Company

Address

Street Address

City   State/Province   Postal/Zip Code

Phone Number   –   –

INVESTMENTS
Information Sheet

INVESTMENT INFORMATION

Type of
Investment

Account
Number

Financial
Institution

Address

Street Address

City

State/Province

Postal/Zip Code

Phone Number   –   –

INVESTMENT INFORMATION

Type of
Investment

Account
Number

Financial
Institution

Address

Street Address

City

State/Province

Postal/Zip Code

Phone Number   –   –

INVESTMENT INFORMATION

Type of
Investment

Account
Number

Financial
Institution

Address

Street Address

City   State/Province   Postal/Zip Code

Phone Number   –   –

INVESTMENT INFORMATION

Type of
Investment

Account
Number

Financial
Institution

Address

Street Address

City   State/Province   Postal/Zip Code

Phone Number   –   –

INVESTMENT INFORMATION

Type of
Investment

Account
Number

Financial
Institution

Address

Street Address

City   State/Province   Postal/Zip Code

Phone Number   –   –

INVESTMENT INFORMATION

Type of
Investment

Account
Number

Financial
Institution

Address

Street Address

City

State/Province

Postal/Zip Code

Phone Number   –   –

INVESTMENT INFORMATION

Type of
Investment

Account
Number

Financial
Institution

Address

Street Address

City

State/Province

Postal/Zip Code

Phone Number   –   –

INVESTMENT INFORMATION

Type of
Investment

Account
Number

Financial
Institution

Address

Street Address

City

State/Province

Postal/Zip Code

Phone Number   –   –

PERSONAL POSSESSIONS INFORMATION

☐ **Pictures on CD**   ☐ **List of Valuables**

☐ **Scanned Receipts
of Big-Ticket Items**

PERSONAL POSSESSIONS INFORMATION

In this section you will document your home and personal possessions.

As I stated in the preface, the advice/information in this section gave me the idea for this organizer. My recommendation is to take extensive pictures of your home and properties. These pictures should include personal possessions of value in each room of your house, including those in closets, the basement, the garage (tools, equipment), the backyard, and so on, and of boats and other recreational vehicles (inside and out). Additionally, find the receipts for your big-screen TV, computer, paintings, camera, video equipment, and so on. Scan these receipts and save the images on a CD with your pictures. Do you have pictures of special items like heirlooms? Do you have pictures of jewelry? Do you have an appraisal on your jewelry or other valuables? Once the pictures are completed and on a CD, keep the CD in a holder in the front of your binder.

See the story below that confirms the need to have this documentation as well as the importance of keeping another binder off premises with a trusted family member or friend who does not live nearby— this second binder should be miles away from the possible disaster that you could experience.

South Lake Tahoe, California—Fire of 2007

I grew up in the San Francisco Bay Area, and one of my favorite places to visit is South Lake Tahoe to stay with our friends who now reside there. On June 24, 2007, my friend called me to tell me that a fire had started less than ten miles away from her home. It was a dry and windy day, with severe fire danger conditions, and in three hours, the fire had spread four miles away from its starting point. The fire left over three thousand acres charred and destroyed over two hundred fifty homes.

We visited this area for the Fourth of July, just a little over a week after the fire was contained, and we were stunned to see the devastation. The area looked like a bomb had gone off. All we could see were charred cars standing on a foundation that used to be a garage, charred washers and dryers standing in what used to be a laundry room, and numerous foundations where beautiful homes had stood. The trees were all burned to a crisp. Those who were home at the time of the fire had only minutes to get their things out; however, most of these residents were not so lucky and could not get all their valuable possessions out of their homes in time.

In the aftermath of this horrible fire, little was salvaged. People told of how they found all of their silverware melted into a hunk and jewelry melted where the jewelry box once stood. People were walking around calling to pets that had run away when the fire came, desperately hoping their pets would return to them. I was heartbroken to see that people had lost everything they owned: their pets, possessions, dreams, and memories. Now I think to myself, with this destruction and loss what could have made it easier for these poor people? I wish they would have left an extra completed *Grab N Go Essential Document Organizer* with a family member or a trusted friend who lived far from the fire. It's most unfortunate they lost everything, but, being an insurance adjuster, I knew that having this information would have made it easier to recuperate most of their losses.

PERSONAL POSSESSIONS

☐ **Personalized photo CD that includes photos of every room in your house.**

- Living room to include paintings, pictures, piano, furniture, figurines, collectibles of value

- Family room to include television, Blu-ray/DVD player, stereo, speakers, furniture, movie cabinet (list of all movies)

- Kitchen/dining room area to include appliances, dining room table, buffet, china hutch, china, kitchen cabinets with pots, pans, dishes, glasses

- Bedrooms to include all bedroom sets, closets with clothing, any valuables

- Master bedroom same as above, but also include pictures of jewelry, family heirlooms, furs

- Closets to include linens and valuables

- Home office to include furniture, computers, TV, cameras, printer/copier

- Laundry room to include washer and dryer

- Garage to include vehicles bicycles, ATVs, lawn mower, yard equipment, tools, any appliances

☐ **Receipts of any big-ticket items.**

☐ **List of your valuables along with description, value, serial number, and appraisal.**

PET INFORMATION

☐ **Pet Information Sheet**

☐ **Animal Emergency Plan**

PET INFORMATION

People who have pets usually worry about their beloved dog, cat, horse, bird, or even favorite mouse or hamster. Animals can also be affected by a major disaster and can end up displaced from their loyal family.

- In this section you will document what kind of animals or pets you have and their names, approximate ages, last immunization shots, pictures, microchip identification numbers, and the veterinarian who is aware of your pets' medical histories.

- In addition to including the above information abut your animals, make a plan of what you would do with your animals in the event of a disaster.

- It is important that you find a place that will board your animals. With the Herriman fires, most people thought they were going to move their animals a few miles east. However, the fire turned for the worse and headed in the same direction as the next shelters. Ultimately, families found that they had to move their animals miles away.

- Make sure your pets have proper IDs and their current vaccination records. Your pets will feel more of the comforts of home when you have their pet carriers and pet supplies.

- Check in advance which local motels and hotels allow animals, in case of an evacuation.

PET
Information Sheet

Name

Approximate
Age

Microchip No.

Other Pet Information

_____
_____
_____
_____

PHOTO

PET INFORMATION

Name

Approximate
Age

Microchip No.

Other Pet Information

_____
_____
_____
_____

PHOTO

PET INFORMATION

Name

Approximate
Age

Microchip No.

Other Pet Information

_____
_____
_____
_____

PHOTO

PET INFORMATION

Name

Approximate
Age

Microchip No.

Other Pet Information

_____

_____

_____

_____

PHOTO

PET INFORMATION

Name

Approximate
Age

Microchip No.

Other Pet Information

_____

_____

_____

_____

PHOTO

VETERINARIAN INFORMATION

Name

Address

Street Address

City   State/Province   Postal/Zip Code

Phone Number   -   -

WILLS AND TRUSTS INFORMATION

☐ **Legal and Guardianship Information Sheet**

☐ **Living Trust**

☐ **Life Insurance Policy**

☐ **Advance Care Plan**

☐ **Letters to Family**

WILLS AND TRUSTS INFORMATION

In this section you will include life insurance and will information, a copy of your living trust, your life insurance policy, your advance care plan, letters to immediate family, and other related life insurance, legal, or guardianship documents. See below why it is important to have these documents in your organizer.

- **Why is it important to have a copy of your living trust?**

  So your estate plan and wishes are available. This ensures that money, managed by a trustee, is set aside and made available to your children when they reach a certain age.

- **Why attach a life insurance policy?**

  To help assist with your funeral expenses, burial costs, and medical bills. It is important to know where this policy is to help with such expenses.

- **Why is it important to have a copy of an advance care plan in this section?**

  So you can share your health care wishes before your passing. This documents whether you want to prolong your life. Advance care planning thoughtfully considers a time when you may not be able to make health care decisions for yourself. An advance care plan can help clarify your values, and it will share with those left behind your last desires and decisions, which could include a DNR (do not resuscitate) form.

- **Include in this section a letter for your spouse and each child in case of your death.**

- **Why is it important to have a list of guardians for your children?**

  Accidents do happen, and parents can die together, leaving minor children behind. Having your wishes written down ensures that, in the event of an emergency, your best interests are met in protecting your children.

GUARDIANSHIP AND LEGAL
Information Sheet
In the case of your death

Name of Guardian
or Guardians

Address

Street Address

City   State/Province   Postal/Zip Code

Phone Number   -   -

ESTATE INFORMATION

Executor of
Your Estate

Address

Street Address

City   State/Province   Postal/Zip Code

Phone Number   -   -

LIFE INSURANCE INFORMATION

Life Insurance
Company

Address

Street Address

City   State/Province   Postal/Zip Code

Phone Number   -   -   Policy Number

FUNERAL PLANNING INFORMATION

- ☐ **Death Certificate Information Sheet**
- ☐ **Life Insurance Information Sheet**
- ☐ **Veteran Information Sheet**
- ☐ **Memorial Instructions**

FUNERAL PLANNING INFORMATION

In this section you will include planning for your funeral, including the information required for a death certificate, veteran information, life insurance information, and memorial instructions.

Ultimately we will all complete our mortal lives, whether it happens abruptly, tragically, or peacefully. In any event, you should have your affairs in order so your family will know what to do you when you leave this life. This section will help you in gathering your last wishes.

My mom has been one of my greatest supporters when it comes to completing this organizer. At one point, we found out that my dad was having major back surgery, and my siblings were concerned about whether he would make it through this medical procedure due to his diabetic issues. Being the oldest child, I started speaking with my mom about life insurance and funeral arrangements, questioning her if any of these arrangements had been made.

My mom basically said all the plans were taken care of. It left me with an uneasy feeling, knowing that I had basically no knowledge of what they wanted and where to find this information to make sure these needs were met.

Some items to consider:

1. **Make decisions prior to death.** Emotions are significantly higher after losing a loved one. This can make it difficult to make sound financial decisions. Preplanning reduces the cost of funeral services by avoiding this emotional overspending. This enables you to customize the services to reflect your values, history, and story. Also, by preplanning you can lock in today's prices, saving thousands of dollars. See your local mortuary for more details.

2. **Choose your funeral.** They can vary in price by thousands of dollars for similar services. Family-owned funeral homes are much less expensive than corporate owned.

3. **Choose the cemetery.** Most cities offer a discounted rate for residents. Remember to look at all of the fees, such as the opening and closing costs, not just the cost of the plot. Private cemeteries are significantly higher priced than city cemeteries.

4. **Know how many copies of the death certificate you will need (see list on next page).**

Places that may require death certificate:

- Life insurance
- Insurance companies
- Social security
- Bank accounts/safe-deposit box (including joint accounts)
- Retirement/pension
- Trusts
- Title company
- Pre-need funeral plan
- Investment brokers/CDs, stocks/bonds
- Credit cards

Additional pre-death planning:

1. Let your children (or whoever will take care of your estate when you pass) know if you have any leased off-site properties or a safe-deposit box and make plans to remove the items and end the lease.

2. Speak with your children or designated trustee about any bills or expenses that will need to be addressed with your passing: any credit cards, home services, cable services, newspaper services, and so on.

Post-death actions:

In the event of your death, your next of kin or trustee should complete the following:

1. Contact the US Postal Service within two days of death to make sure that mail is forwarded to a responsible party. Keep in mind, in the event of a death, people watch for obituaries and look to either rob the house where the decedent lived or take their mail, in which they would have had social security checks delivered.

2. File claims with life insurance and annuity companies and notify insurance companies to terminate coverages.

3. Contact employer about 401(k), pension, or company benefits to which the decedent may be entitled.

4. Notify the Social Security Administration to discuss further benefits.

5. Remove decedent's name from any known marketing and mailing lists and place name on do-not-contact lists.

6. Contact the DMV to cancel the decedent's driver's license.

7. Discuss any pending, unfiled tax returns with the accountant.

8. Order numerous copies of death certificates.

DEATH CERTIFICATE
Information Sheet

First Name _____   Middle Name _____

Last Name _____

Address _____
Street Address

City _____   State/Province _____   Postal/Zip Code _____

Phone Number ___ - ___ - ___   Cell Phone ___ - ___ - ___

Email _____   Date of Birth ___ - ___ - ___

Place of Birth _____
City   County

Occupation _____   Employer _____
If retired, list most recent employer

Education _____   Social Security Number ___ - ___ - ___

Marital Status _____   Spouse's Name _____

Marriage Date ___ - ___ - ___

Previous Spouse _____   Marriage Date ___ - ___ - ___

Father's Name _____   Mother's Maiden Name _____

Father Deceased   Y / N   Mother Deceased   Y / N

Will in Place   Y / N   Location _____

Family Living Trust   Y / N   Location _____

Safe-Deposit Box   Y / N   Location _____

VETERAN
Information Sheet

Service Number

Entry Date   -   -

Rank

Separation
Date   -   -

Branch of
Service

LIFE INSURANCE
Information Sheet

Company Name

Location

MEMORIAL INSTRUCTIONS

Below you will document funeral arrangements that have been made prior to your passing.
I would recommend at least two separate documents—one for each parent.

Funeral Home
Name

Address

Street Address

City   State/Province   Postal/Zip Code

Phone
Number   _   _   _

Person in
Charge of   Relation
Arrangements   to You

Address

Street Address

City   State/Province   Postal/Zip Code

Phone
Number   _   _   _

Religious
Denomination   Clergy

Disposition Preference   Burial   Mausoleum   Entombment   Cremation

Memorial Service
Location   Church   Funeral Home   Graveside   Other _____

Viewing
Arrangements   Church   Funeral Home   None

Casket   Open   Closed

Obituary   Y / N   Photo   Y / N

Participating Fraternal, Military, or Service Organization

Music

Speakers

Casket Spray Preference

Casket Preference

Vault Preference

Additional Requests and Instructions

_____

_____

_____

_____

_____

_____

_____

_____

_____

_____

_____

CEMETERY INSTRUCTIONS

Cemetery Property Owned   Y / N   Marker Owned   Y / N

Cemetery Name

Address

    Street Address

    City

Phone
Number   –   –

Section/Garden
Location   Lot   Space

Cremation
Memorialization   Niche   Burial   Other _____

Additional Requests and Instructions

_____
_____
_____
_____
_____
_____
_____
_____
_____
_____
_____

EMERGENCY PLANS

☐ **State Emergency Plan**

☐ **Local Emergency Plan**

☐ **Family Emergency Plan**

EMERGENCY PLANS

In this section you will place your state, local, and family emergency plans.
Please note that most states follow the FEMA emergency guidelines.

For state and federal emergency plans, one of the most popular websites is

www.ready.gov

Be Informed: Know what to do before, during, and after an emergency occurs.

Make a plan: Develop a plan around the locations you frequent the most, such as home, school, work, and church.

Local Emergency Plans:

I recommend contacting the city offices where you live to request a copy of their local emergency plan.

Family Emergency Plans:

When it comes to a disaster, your family may not be together, so plan in advance how you will contact each other, how you will get back together, and what to do in different situations.

Contacts:

In the event of an emergency, more than likely it will be easier to contact someone who lives out of state versus locally. Make sure that each family member knows the phone number and is able to contact this person. Have emergency cards in wallets or backpacks.

Work and School:

Review disaster plans for your work and your children's schools.

Escape Routes and Meeting Place:

Determine two escape routes from each room in your house. Determine escape routes from your home to a designated neighborhood meeting place. This could be a local school, church, friend's home, or city office building.

Children:

Teach them how and when to call 9-1-1 and other emergency numbers.

EMERGENCY FUNDS

☐ **On-hand Cash**

EMERGENCY FUNDS

In this section I recommend that you put hundreds of dollars in small bills in a large manila envelope, as an emergency fund. If a major disaster takes place, you will more than likely not be able to use credit cards or an ATM because the machines will be down. Years ago, my family in Michigan were without power for days due to ice storms. So no power equals no ATMs for cash. If you *are* able to buy food or fuel, it will most likely be on a cash-only basis. You should keep tens and twenties versus one-hundred-dollar bills. In a crisis, you won't find change for large bills.

MISCELLANEOUS

☐ **Computer Information Sheet**

☐ **Household Codes**

☐ **Other Documents**

COMPUTER
Information Sheet

PERSONAL EMAIL INFORMATION

Email Address

Username   Password

Email Address

Username   Password

Email Address

Username   Password

Email Address

Username   Password

WORK EMAIL INFORMATION

Email Address

Username   Password

SOCIAL MEDIA INFORMATION

Facebook

Username   Password

Twitter

Username   Password

Pinterest

Username   Password

OTHER WEBSITE INFORMATION

Website/Account

Username   Password

Website/Account

Username   Password

Website/Account

Username   Password

Website/Account

Username   Password

HOUSEHOLD CODES

Household Alarm
Code

Garage Code

Home Phone
Number

_ _ _

Voicemail

_ _ _

Password

Additional Information

_____
_____
_____
_____
_____
_____
_____
_____
_____
_____
_____
_____
_____
_____
_____
_____
_____
_____
_____
_____
_____

CPSIA information can be obtained
at www.ICGtesting.com
Printed in the USA
BVHW010806270420
578600BV00010B/102